# The Ancient World

Written by Zoë Clarke

Illustrated by Alejandro Mila

RISING ★ STARS

# Back in time

Do you think the people who lived in the past were different from us? They may not have had the things we have today, such as mobile phones and computers, but they found new ways of doing things all the time.

Each page in this book has a timeline. The timeline tells you when different people were alive.

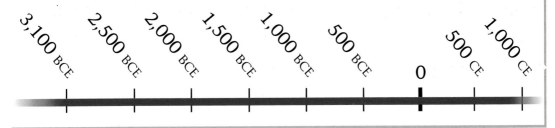

3,100 BCE  2,500 BCE  2,000 BCE  1,500 BCE  1,000 BCE  500 BCE  0  500 CE  1,000 CE

The map shows you where in the world these people lived.

The photographs and drawings show you the amazing things that happened in the **ancient** world.

# Stone Age people

3.4 million years ago                    2,500 BCE

What were people doing millions of years ago?

The most important thing was to stay alive. Stone Age people hunted and gathered food. They used a hard stone called flint to make weapons and tools.

This piece of sharpened flint was used as an axe.

Life was hard, but it wasn't all work for Stone Age people. They painted pictures of animals and people on cave walls. They also left handprints.

Some handprints were made by blowing paint around a hand. The paint was made of different coloured rocks crushed together.

# Bronze Age people

2,500 BCE                         800 BCE

Bronze Age people still used stone,
but now they had a new material.
Bronze was brought to Britain
from Europe and everyone liked it!

Britain

Bronze was made into all kinds of useful things. Warriors fought with sharp swords and spears made of bronze. They wore bronze helmets and held bronze shields.

Look how different this axe is from the Stone Age axe.

Not everything was made of bronze. During the Bronze Age people learned to weave and make clothes from wool. They also made pottery, which may have been used to hold food and drink at feasts.

Some Bronze Age pots were decorated with patterns.

# The Shang and the Zhou

1,500 BCE                           481 BCE

Two of the most important families who ruled in Ancient China were called the Shang and the Zhou.

Modern China

Shang and Zhou

When the Shang ruled China, people found a new way of turning bronze into useful things. They poured **molten** bronze into hollow containers, called moulds. These moulds could be taken apart and used again.

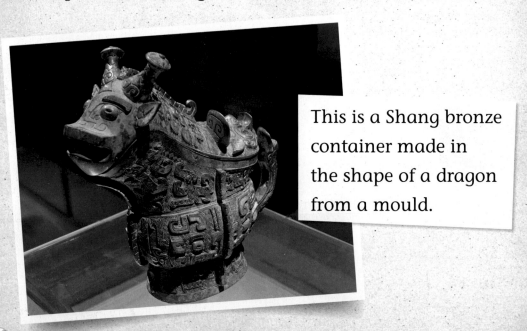

This is a Shang bronze container made in the shape of a dragon from a mould.

The Shang used shells as money. By the time the Zhou ruled Ancient China, coins had been invented. Bronze coins weren't round; they came in different shapes – like fish!

The Zhou defended their land by building walls of earth to keep their enemies out. Later, the Great Wall of China was built on top of these walls.

# The Olmec people

1,200 BCE                                   400 BCE

The Olmec people built huge buildings called pyramids. Olmec pyramids were made of large blocks of stone and they had steps going up the sides. Important Olmecs would climb the steps to the top.

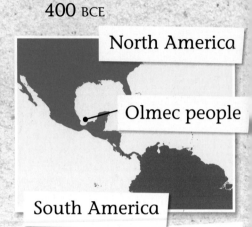

North America

Olmec people

South America

Along with big buildings, the Olmec people also liked big art! They **carved** giant heads out of stone, but no one's quite sure why. The heads are all different and they may show important Olmec leaders.

This Olmec man is wearing a hat.

# The Ancient Egyptians

3,100 BCE                             330 BCE

Like the Olmecs, the Ancient Egyptians also built pyramids, which were made of huge blocks of stone. Some pyramids took years to build. Pyramids were **tombs** for their leaders, called pharaohs.

Egypt

There are about 2.3 million stone blocks in the Great Pyramid of Giza!

The Ancient Egyptians liked metal too. They made beautiful things like jewellery out of copper, silver, gold, iron, lead and bronze.

The Ancient Egyptians wrote on paper made out of plants, called papyrus. They also carved on stone. The Ancient Egyptians used pictures and **symbols**. These are called hieroglyphs. (Say 'high-roe-gliffs'.)

# The Ancient Greeks

800 BCE    500 BCE

Greece was an exciting place to be in the ancient world.

The Ancient Greeks built huge **temples**, invented the theatre and wrote lots of plays and poetry. The first ever Olympic Games were held in Greece, where the winners won a crown made of olive branches.

Greece

This large temple is called the Acropolis.

The Ancient Greeks also had their own alphabet.

The Ancient Greeks had lots of good ideas. A man called Aristotle thought the Earth was round, but at the time, no one believed him!

The Ancient Greeks made lots of new rules and laws. In some Greek cities, some of the people were allowed to choose who would become their ruler. This idea spread to other parts of the world.

# Iron Age people

800 BCE                                    45 CE

Meanwhile … in Britain people still couldn't write, but there were lots of other things going on.

Britain

A new metal was brought to Britain. As well as bronze, people could now make things out of iron. Iron is much sharper than bronze, and it made better weapons and tools.

Iron Age people farmed the land and they lived in roundhouses like this.

Iron Age people also built hillforts. These forts were built on the top of hills and may have protected people from attack.

high wooden fence

ditches

Ditches made it more difficult for enemies to get into the hillfort.

# The Ancient Romans

509 BCE · · · · · 476 CE

Rome was the most powerful place in the ancient world.

This huge building is called the Colosseum. It was built to show everyone how important the rulers in Rome were.

Italy

Inside the Colosseum, Romans watched warriors and wild animals fight. There were seats for 50,000 people!

# How did Rome become so powerful?

The Romans had a large army, which was bigger than anyone else's. Their soldiers were well trained and won lots of battles. When Romans **defeated** their enemies, they took their land.

The Romans were also great inventors. They built huge channels, called aqueducts, to move water from one place to another. This aqueduct in France was built in Roman times.

# The Maya people

200 BCE                                                900 CE

The Maya people lived in cities surrounded by forests. They also built huge pyramids made of stone. The Maya pyramids were temples. Maya kings climbed the steps to the top of the pyramid and gave gifts to their gods.

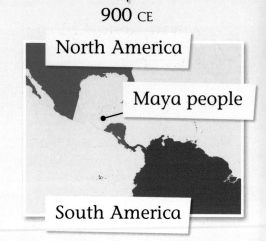

North America

Maya people

South America

There are buildings at the top.

steps

20

The Maya people played a game called pok-a-tok, which is a bit like football.

| How many teams played? | Two |
|---|---|
| Number of players | Any number |
| What do you need? | One rubber ball |
| How long was the game? | It could go on for days! |
| How do you score? | Touch special markers with the ball |
| | Get the ball through the hole in the markers |
| What happens if you lose? | You die! |

a pok-a-tok marker

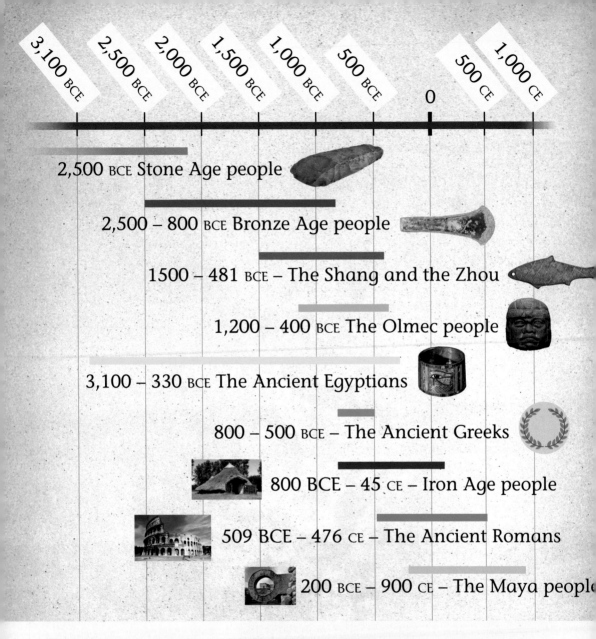

3,100 BCE    2,500 BCE    2,000 BCE    1,500 BCE    1,000 BCE    500 BCE    0    500 CE    1,000 CE

2,500 BCE Stone Age people

2,500 – 800 BCE Bronze Age people

1500 – 481 BCE – The Shang and the Zhou

1,200 – 400 BCE The Olmec people

3,100 – 330 BCE The Ancient Egyptians

800 – 500 BCE – The Ancient Greeks

800 BCE – 45 CE – Iron Age people

509 BCE – 476 CE – The Ancient Romans

200 BCE – 900 CE – The Maya people

The ancient world was full of new and exciting ideas. Look around at the world today, and you will see that people are still inventing and building – thinking of better ways to do things – just like the people of the ancient world.

# Glossary

**ancient**        in a time long past

**carved**        to shape with a sharp tool

**defeated**        beat someone in battle

**molten**        metal that is heated so it becomes liquid

**symbols**        drawn signs instead of words

**temple**        a place to worship

**tombs**        graves

# Talk about the book

Answer the questions:

1 What did Stone Age people use to make paint?

2 What did the Shang use as money?

3 Where were the first ever Olympic Games held?

4 Can you think of another word that means the same as 'defeated'? (page 19)

5 Why were the Romans so good at beating other people in battle?

6 Which ancient people built pyramids?

7 Explain why Iron Age people built hillforts on top of hills.

8 Would you like to play a game of pok-a-tok like the Maya people? Why or why not?